Original title:
The Heart's Commitment



Author: Johan Kirsipuu
ISBN HARDBACK: 978-9916-89-319-7
ISBN PAPERBACK: 978-9916-89-320-3
ISBN EBOOK: 978-9916-89-321-0

## Underneath the Same Moon

Underneath the same moon, we stand,
Whispers of dreams shared, hand in hand.
Stars twinkle softly, a guiding light,
Illuminating love through the night.

In silence we speak, our hearts in tune,
Dancing shadows cast by the moon.
Time moves slowly, yet swiftly it flies,
Beneath this vast canvas, our spirits rise.

Every heartbeat echoes, a timeless song,
Together in stillness, where we belong.
With every breath, a promise so true,
Underneath the same moon, me and you.

## Reflections of Shared Futures

In the mirror of time, we see our paths,
Woven together, in life's aftermaths.
Bright visions glimmer, in twilight's embrace,
Reflecting our hopes, a destined place.

Futures entwined like vines on a wall,
Holding each other, we rise when we fall.
Through trials faced and storms we brace,
Together we shine, a radiant grace.

In the tapestry of life, our threads unite,
Crafting a journey, both bold and bright.
With each step forward, we'll boldly strive,
Reflections of shared futures, we thrive.

## Threads of the Same Fabric

In the loom of existence, we stitch our dreams,
Threads of the same fabric, stronger than seams.
Colors entwined in a beautiful blend,
Together we rise, on each other we depend.

Each moment we capture, a knot to tie,
Binding aspirations as high as the sky.
With laughter woven into our design,
In this pattern of time, your heart is mine.

Through storms and sun, the fabric we weave,
In the warmth of our bond, we believe.
Together forever, through love's endless glow,
Threads of the same fabric, together we grow.

## A Promise Against the Tide

As the waves crash fierce on the rugged shore,
A promise against the tide, forevermore.
With every heartbeat, the love we hold,
Stands unwavering, a story bold.

Drifting sands may shift, but our vows stay true,
In the face of the storm, it's me and you.
With every sunrise, a chance to renew,
A pledge to stand firm, in all that we do.

In the dance of the sea, we find our way,
Navigating together, come what may.
Against the tide, our spirits ignite,
A promise everlasting, fully in sight.

## Under the Canopy of Vows

Beneath the leaves, we stand together,
Whispers of love in the gentle tether.
Promises made, with hearts so bright,
Wrapped in the warmth of a starlit night.

Each branch a witness, each root a sign,
As we entwine in the sacred pine.
Seasons will change, yet we'll remain,
In the shelter of vows, through joy and pain.

The sun may fade, the rain may fall,
Yet here we'll build, through it all.
The vibrant hues of life we paint,
In this sacred space where no love is faint.

The canopy thick, with dreams ablaze,
We craft our story in countless ways.
With laughter and tears, our spirits soar,
Under the vows, forevermore.

In every rustle, we hear the call,
Together in silence, we capture it all.
Hand in hand, we'll face the dawn,
Under this canopy, our love lives on.

## A Circle Unbroken

In the heart of the dance, the laughter flows,
Spinning together as the moonlight glows.
Each step a bond, a spark of grace,
In a circle unbroken, we find our place.

Time whispers softly, yet hearts are bold,
Stories of love and friendship unfold.
The rhythm of life in every beat,
A melody sweet, where souls do meet.

From seasons of joy to trials faced,
In this circle, no moment's misplaced.
The warmth of your hand, the light in your eyes,
Together we rise, beneath endless skies.

With laughter and tears, we journey on,
Hand in hand, as the night turns to dawn.
In stillness we gather, in love we trust,
A circle unbroken, forever a must.

So here we stand, in the glow of the fire,
Bound by the love that never will tire.
In the circle we share, our spirits will thrive,
For in this connection, together, we're alive.

## Lanterns Lit in Affection

In the dark, they softly glow,
Casting warmth where love can flow.
Each flicker tells a story bright,
Of hearts entwined in endless night.

Guiding souls through unseen ways,
Brightening the longest days.
Together, we will light the sky,
With lanterns lit, our spirits fly.

With each flame, a promise made,
In gentle whispers, fears will fade.
Let's cherish this glowing tether,
Lanterns shine, we shine together.

## Rivers of Resilient Connection

Beneath the surface, deep they flow,
Rivers of bonds we come to know.
With every ripple, love remains,
Through stormy skies and gentle rains.

In currents strong, we feel the beat,
Together, rising, never defeat.
The water sings of trust so true,
In every drop, I find you too.

Winding paths that twist and turn,
In harmony, our spirits yearn.
Through valleys wide and hills so steep,
In rivers deep, our promises keep.

## A Tapestry of Trust and Dreams

In colors bright, our stories weave,
A tapestry of hopes to cleave.
Threads of trust, so strong and fine,
Intertwined, our fates align.

Each stitch a moment, bold and bright,
Transforming darkness into light.
Dreams embossed on every strand,
Together we will always stand.

As patterns form, we share our fears,
In woven whispers, love appears.
A work of art, both rich and deep,
In this tapestry, our souls will leap.

## Seeds of Promises Planted Deep

In quiet soil, our dreams take root,
Seeds of hope in every foot.
With gentle hands, we nurture care,
In sunlight's warmth, our spirits share.

As tender buds begin to bloom,
Life unfurls, dispelling gloom.
Promises made with every sprout,
In gardens wide, we journey out.

Through seasons' change, we stand with pride,
In this rich earth, we will abide.
With time and trust, we'll reap the sweep,
In love's embrace, our dreams run deep.

## The Lattice of Lifelong Love

In the garden where hearts entwine,
Every moment shared, a sweet design.
Woven paths of laughter and tears,
A tapestry built through the years.

Hands held tightly in storm and sun,
Two souls united, forever one.
Each thread a promise, soft yet strong,
In this lattice, we both belong.

Through seasons of change, we bloom and fade,
In shadows and light, foundations laid.
A home built on dreams and trust so true,
In this lattice, it's me and you.

Memories etched like flowers in clay,
Each petal a whisper of yesterday.
With every glance, love's warmth ignites,
A guiding star in the darkest nights.

At the core of this life we weave,
The gift of love is what we believe.
In the lattice of lifelong grace,
Together we find our sacred space.

## Whispers of Devotion

In quiet moments, secrets unfold,
Soft vows exchanged, more precious than gold.
A gentle touch, a knowing glance,
In whispers of love, we find our chance.

Every heartbeat a symphony plays,
In dance of romance, lost in the maze.
Through trials faced, we stand in grace,
In whispers of devotion, we find our place.

The sun may set, yet stars will rise,
In the velvet sky, our dreams disguise.
Each low murmur, a promise made,
In love’s embrace, our worries fade.

Even in silence, our souls connect,
In the simplest moments, love's perfect effect.
Through gentle words, our spirits soar,
In whispers of devotion, forevermore.

Together we walk, hand in hand,
Through winding paths in this shared land.
In every breath, our stories sing,
In whispers of love, hope takes wing.

## Ties of Unbreakable Trust

In the maze of life, we find our way,
With every promise, come what may.
Through darkness and light, we navigate,
In ties of trust, we elevate.

With eyes wide open, we dream wide,
In the depths of the heart, we confide.
Each secret shared, a bond we grow,
In these ties, our love will flow.

Challenges faced, side by side,
With hands held high, we will abide.
In the storms of life, we'll stand tall,
In ties of trust, we conquer all.

Every sigh exchanged, a sacred pact,
In the silence, we find the act.
A fortress built with tender stone,
In ties of trust, we are never alone.

With laughter and tears, we find our truth,
Bound by the essence of eternal youth.
Together we soar, brave and free,
In ties of unbreakable trust, just you and me.

## Reflections in Still Waters

Beneath the sky, the waters gleam,
A mirror holds a silent dream.
Ripples dance, the shadows play,
Whispers of night consume the day.

Trees sway gently, secrets flow,
In this moment, time moves slow.
Clouds drift by, a canvas bright,
Nature's heart in tranquil light.

Footsteps fade on the soft shore,
Echoes linger, forevermore.
Each glance held in the tranquil glass,
Moments caught, they never pass.

In quietude, the world retreats,
Where peace and water softly meet.
Reflections deep, beyond the vine,
In stillness, all our hearts entwine.

## A Symphony of Binding Love

Two hearts beat in a soft refrain,
A melody sweet, dancing in vain.
Hands united, a gentle touch,
In this harmony, we find so much.

With every note, a promise made,
Through every storm, we will not fade.
In laughter's song, in sorrow's hum,
A symphony plays, forever thrum.

Eyes meet gently, sparks ignite,
A candle's glow in the quiet night.
In whispered dreams, our futures blend,
A love's refrain, that shall not end.

Together strong, we storm the skies,
In every challenge, love will rise.
A binding force, both fierce and sweet,
In this duet, our souls complete.

## Stone and Feather: Unbreakable Features

In mountains high, the stones declare,
Their grounded strength, beyond compare.
Yet on the breeze, the feathers glide,
A dance of grace, with nature's pride.

Two different worlds, a bond so rare,
The weight of earth, the light in air.
Together they form a vivid frame,
A story told, in nature's name.

Through trials faced, they stand as one,
Unbreakable ties, tightly spun.
The stone provides what feathers lack,
In harmony, they share the track.

Roots can anchor, winds can soar,
Balance found at the ocean's shore.
In every form, they intertwine,
A dance of fate, by grand design.

## The Echo of Tides and Time

Waves crash softly, the shore's embrace,
An endless rhythm, a timeless race.
The tide pulls forth, then retreats away,
Marking moments of each day.

Footprints left in the soaking sand,
Fleeting traces of love so grand.
As waters rise, then fall with grace,
Life's ebb and flow we all must face.

Whispers of ages in the breeze,
Secrets hidden in the trees.
The sun dips low, a crimson glow,
Where memories fade, but love will grow.

Each crash of wave, a tale in time,
A symphony carved in ancient rhyme.
As seasons change and moments blend,
The echoes of tides will never end.

## The Fire That Never Fades

In the heart, it softly glows,
A warmth that time cannot impose.
Memories dance like flames in night,
An ember’s pulse, a guiding light.

Through stormy seas and trials grim,
Our spirits rise, they will not dim.
Together forged in passion's blaze,
Love ignites in countless ways.

The echoes of our laughter bright,
Illuminate the darkest night.
With every spark, a promise made,
The fire that never will evade.

Though winds may howl and shadows loom,
We find our way, dispelling gloom.
In every challenge, bond remains,
The fire, forever, sustains.

So let it burn, this sacred flame,
In joy or sorrow, still the same.
A testament, our hearts displayed,
In love’s embrace, we are arrayed.

## Elysian Bonds

In fields where dreams and whispers blend,
We find a path that has no end.
Each touch, a promise softly sown,
In sacred ground, our love has grown.

Through seasons' change and gentle breeze,
We walk as one beneath the trees.
With every glance, our souls align,
A harmony by fate designed.

Stars above in silent gaze,
Bear witness to our endless praise.
Together, hearts in perfect rhyme,
Elysian bonds that transcend time.

In laughter shared and tears we shed,
Our journey weaves, where love is bred.
With every heartbeat strong and free,
We celebrate our destiny.

Though trials come and shadows fall,
Together we shall stand through all.
In fervent trust, we take our stand,
Elysian bonds, forever hand in hand.

## Portraits of Togetherness

In frames of joy, we capture light,
A canvas painted with delight.
Each smile a brushstroke, bold and true,
Portraits of love, forever new.

With colors bright, the moments blend,
In gentle hues, our spirits mend.
A tapestry of laughter shared,
In every stitch, our hearts have bared.

Through every storm, we find our song,
A melody that carries on.
In echoes of our whispered dreams,
Together we're more than what it seems.

In twilight's glow, our shadows cast,
Reflecting futures, holding fast.
A gallery of life unveiled,
In love, our stories are detailed.

So let us frame each passing day,
In every glance and word we say.
Together, in this life we strive,
Portraits of togetherness, alive.

## Sails of Resilience

With winds of change, we set our course,
Navigating life with steady force.
Through tempests fierce and skies so gray,
Our sails of resilience pave the way.

In turbulent seas, our spirits soar,
With unity, we find the shore.
Each challenge met, a wave we ride,
Together strong, we turn the tide.

Anchored deep in trust, we stand,
Through rocky paths, we hold each hand.
With every gust, our courage grows,
In harmony, our promise flows.

We chart our path with hope aglow,
No storm too fierce, no wave too low.
With hearts as one, we face the fight,
Sails of resilience, guiding light.

Through horizons wide and stars aligned,
Our journey echoes, hope entwined.
On this great voyage, side by side,
Sails of resilience, our true guide.

**Unseen Threads of Togetherness**

In silence, we weave our dreams,
A tapestry of whispered themes.
Though miles apart, we hold so tight,
Unseen threads connect our light.

The laughter shared, the tears we shed,
In every word, the love we've bred.
Through trials faced, we find our way,
Together, come what may.

Like stars aligned in night’s embrace,
Our hearts entwined in sacred space.
An echo of vows, soft and clear,
In every heartbeat, you are near.

Through storms of doubt, we stay as one,
A dance of shadows, just begun.
In every challenge, strength we find,
The bond we share, forever blind.

So cherish the moments, small and grand,
In life’s great journey, hand in hand.
With unseen threads, we'll never part,
Together forever, heart to heart.

## Portraits of Pledged Souls

Two figures brushed in colors bright,
Captured in frames, love's pure light.
With every glance, a story told,
Of hearts entwined, and spirits bold.

In quiet corners, dreams collide,
With whispers soft, where hopes abide.
The promises made, like banners high,
In portraits painted 'neath the sky.

A journey shared, with paths aligned,
Each scar a testament, love refined.
In every smile, a vow remains,
Through laughter shared, and hidden pains.

With open arms, we face the dawn,
In love’s embrace, we are reborn.
The canvas stretches, colors blend,
In timeless strokes, our hearts transcend.

Through trials faced, together strong,
In every note, our hearts belong.
These portraits hold what words can't say,
In silent whispers, love finds a way.

## Emblems of Unshakable Bonds

In every glance, a promise lies,
A strength that never fades or dies.
Together forged through fire and pain,
Unshakable bonds, a true refrain.

With every heartbeat, faith we share,
In quiet moments, love laid bare.
Through storms that threaten, we will stand,
With steadfast hearts and open hands.

Like trees entwined, we touch the sky,
With roots that deepen, never shy.
In sunlight's glow or shadowed gloom,
Our spirits rise, forever bloom.

Through trials faced and joys embraced,
In every memory, love interlaced.
These emblems of trust in hearts we hold,
A sacred story, forever told.

So let us dance in life's embrace,
With every step, we find our place.
Together forged, a bond so strong,
In unshakable love, we belong.

## Navigating Through Life's Storms

With sails unfurled, we brave the night,
Against the winds, we seek the light.
With every wave that threatens to break,
Together, we find the strength to wake.

Through thunder's roar and lightning's flash,
In turbulent seas, our hopes we stash.
In every storm, a lesson learned,
With passion's fire, our souls are burned.

Our compass set on dreams we share,
With love as guide, we face the dare.
Through rocky shores and tempest's howl,
In unity's strength, we'll take a bow.

When shadows linger and doubts arise,
In each other's arms, we'll synthesize.
With whispered prayers and steadfast grace,
We navigate, our sacred space.

As dawn unfurls her golden light,
We chart our course, prepared for flight.
Through life's storms, a journey vast,
Together we sail, our friendships cast.

## Love's Unbreakable Thread

In the quiet moments bright,
Hearts entwined, they softly sigh.
Through storms and skies of grey,
Together they will always stay.

Each promise made, a binding tie,
A woven path beneath the sky.
In every glance, a world anew,
With love's embrace, they journey through.

Time may change, seasons may shift,
Yet love persists, a timeless gift.
In laughter shared and tears shed,
Their souls are sewn, forever wed.

Hand in hand, they face the dawn,
With whispered dreams, the night is gone.
Through trials faced, they only grow,
In love's warm light, their spirits glow.

So here's to hearts that beat as one,
In every shadow, in each sun.
Love's unbreakable thread shall last,
In every future, as in the past.

## Whispers of Endless Devotion

In the hush of twilight's glow,
Soft whispers dance, a gentle flow.
Promises linger on the breeze,
In every heart, a sacred ease.

Words unspoken, yet clearly felt,
In every touch, the warmth is dealt.
A language known to only two,
In every glance, devotion true.

Through life's winding, endless road,
They share the weight, they share the load.
In laughter's ring and silence deep,
Their love a treasure, theirs to keep.

With every sunrise, hope renewed,
In shaded paths, their love pursued.
In tender nights, under starry skies,
The whispers hold what never dies.

Together through the tides of time,
In every beat, their hearts align.
With endless devotion, they ascend,
In every moment, love's own blend.

## Roots Beneath the Surface

In the soil where secrets lie,
Roots entwined, they ever tie.
Beneath the earth, their strength does bind,
A love that flourishes, unconfined.

Through seasons change, they hold the ground,
In silent whispers, love is found.
Though storms may rage and winds may howl,
Their bonds grow deeper, strong and foul.

In shadows cast, their tendrils weave,
A tapestry of what they believe.
In every struggle, every strain,
They rise together, love's refrain.

As flowers bloom and colors gleam,
Their roots run deep, fulfilling dreams.
In life's embrace, they seek the sun,
Together as one, they have begun.

In harmony with earth and sky,
Their love, a treasure, will not die.
With roots beneath, they shall withstand,
A testament of love so grand.

## Flames that Never Fade

In the hearth where embers glow,
Two hearts ignite, a steady flow.
With whispered flames that dance and leap,
A passion fierce, a bond so deep.

Through trials faced and shadows cast,
Their light remains, a flame steadfast.
No winter's chill could ever snuff,
This fire bright, forever tough.

In quiet moments, sparks will fly,
A warmth that lifts, that never dies.
With every laugh, with every tear,
The flames grow strong, year after year.

And in the night, when stars align,
Their love burns bright, a sacred sign.
In every heartbeat, every breath,
They tend the flame, defying death.

So let the world around them change,
Their love shall glow, forever strange.
In every setback and parade,
They tend their hearts, flames never fade.

## An Unseen Tapestry

Threads of life weave through the air,
Colors blend in rich despair.
Moments lost, yet somehow near,
Whispers tell what we hold dear.

Each stitch holds a hidden tale,
Fragile dreams that softly sail.
In shadows cast by time's embrace,
We find our strength, we find our place.

Patterns dance in quiet grace,
Emotions twine, a warm embrace.
Woven hearts in silent trust,
In this fabric, dreams are just.

Time may pull, but threads won't break,
In this weave, the truth we make.
Together, we are intertwined,
A masterpiece of humankind.

Through the loops of joy and pain,
Life's bright colors softly rain.
In this unseen, vibrant scheme,
We stitch the fabric of a dream.

## In the Garden of Promises

Among the blooms, hope's gentle light,
Whispers of dreams that take to flight.
Each petal soft, each fragrance sweet,
In this garden, our hearts meet.

Promises grow like vines that climb,
Through the seasons, marked by time.
Roots entwined beneath the earth,
Sprout of love, a testament of worth.

With every rain, new life appears,
Joyful laughter, shedding fears.
Sunlight dances on dewy leaves,
In this space, the spirit cleaves.

Butterflies flit from bud to bud,
Painting dreams in vibrant flood.
Moments shared in gentle grace,
Here in the garden, we find our place.

As twilight falls, the stars align,
In this garden, hearts entwine.
A place of hope, a sacred theme,
Where love blooms eternal, like a dream.

## Guardians of the Unspoken

Words unsaid hang in the air,
Silent stories beyond compare.
In the shadows, hearts confide,
Guardians stand, side by side.

Echoes linger in the night,
Whispers veiled from mortal sight.
Through silence, we learn to feel,
The weight of truths we conceal.

Eyes convey what lips may hide,
In the quiet, we confide.
Each glance a promise, soft and rare,
In this moment, love laid bare.

Trust the silence, let it guide,
In the stillness, dreams abide.
With gentle hearts, we navigate,
Through unspoken, we create.

As dawn breaks, the words may flow,
Together, we have come to know.
In the stillness, we ignite,
Guardians of love, shining bright.

## The Dance of Togetherness

In moonlight's glow, we find our beat,
Two souls weaving, hearts in heat.
With every step, our shadows play,
In this rhythm, we drift away.

Hands entwined, a sacred space,
Time slows down in this embrace.
Laughter twirls in joyful spins,
The dance begins as the music spins.

Each heartbeat echoes, steady and strong,
Together we've known where we belong.
With grace we move, faces aglow,
In this dance, our spirits flow.

Through highs and lows, we sway as one,
Underneath the setting sun.
In harmony, we lose all fear,
The dance of love always draws near.

As night unfolds, we'll never part,
The dance continues, two beating hearts.
In togetherness, we find our way,
As the stars above begin to play.

## Timeless Echoes

In the stillness of night,
Whispers travel through time.
Memories softly ignite,
Dancing like stars that chime.

Each heartbeat carries the past,
Waves of laughter break the dark.
Moments, too precious to last,
In the silence, find the spark.

Voices linger in the air,
Stories woven with a thread.
Fragments of love and despair,
In their depths, we are led.

As shadows curl and unwind,
Echoes reach across the years.
In the heart, we will find,
The richness held in our tears.

Beneath the moon's gentle gaze,
Life's tapestry takes its shape.
In timelessness, we spend days,
Each glance, a cherished escape.

## In the Shelter of Your Soul

When the world feels cold and bare,
I seek the warmth that you bring.
In the depths of your soft care,
I find solace as I cling.

A refuge from storms that rage,
Where the heart learns to be free.
In each tender, loving page,
I write our own symphony.

In your arms, I find my peace,
Every moment, pure and true.
As the worries gently cease,
I feel the love we imbue.

Through the dark of night we roam,
Hand in hand, we walk as one.
In your eyes, I've found my home,
Together, we greet the sun.

In the shelter of your soul,
I discover who I am.
With your heart as my only goal,
Together, we make life grand.

## Embraced by Eternity

Beneath the stars, we take flight,
Floating on whispers of dreams.
In the embrace of the night,
Everything's closer than seems.

Time dissolves in gentle touch,
Moments stretched beyond the hour.
Every heartbeat means so much,
Love ignites our hidden power.

In the dance of souls entwined,
We traverse the paths of fate.
Every glance, a thread that binds,
Creating our own world of late.

As horizons softly blend,
In the stillness, we do sway.
With each kiss, a timeless trend,
Guiding us on this sweet way.

Embraced by the light of grace,
Infinite love, a sacred space.
In this union, we find place,
Together, we dare to chase.

## The Road We Travel Together

With every step, we unite,
Footprints carved in sand and stone.
Through both day and silent night,
In your heart, I've always known.

The road ahead may twist and bend,
Yet our spirits boldly soar.
Every moment we will spend,
Is a promise to explore.

Through valleys deep and mountains high,
Hand in hand, we face the tide.
Underneath the endless sky,
By your side, I will abide.

As laughter echoes in the breeze,
And the sun paints skies with gold,
In our hearts, there's sweetest ease,
Together, we face the bold.

Each adventure lays the ground,
In the whispers of our song.
Through the journey, joy is found,
On this road, we both belong.

## A Pledge in Gentle Tides

In the cradle of the sea,
Waves whisper soft, and free.
A promise carved in sand,
Eternal, hand in hand.

With the moon's gentle grace,
We find our sacred space.
Each ebb and flow a vow,
Together, here and now.

Though storms may rise and swell,
In your heart, I will dwell.
Our love, a guiding star,
Shining bright, near or far.

As the tides pull and sway,
I pledge my heart each day.
Through the currents, I’ll stay true,
With the ocean, me and you.

In the silence of the night,
We'll dance in silver light.
A bond that will remain,
In the bliss of soft refrain.

## The Latent Flame of Loyalty

In the shadows of the heart,
Burns a flame, a sacred art.
Quiet, yet fiercely bright,
Guiding through the darkest night.

A bond that time won't sever,
In every storm, we endeavor.
Holding fast through winds that blow,
Together, we shall grow.

Silent vows in every glance,
A loyalty, a soulful dance.
In moments rare and sweet,
Our spirits intertwine, complete.

Though distance may arise,
In dreams, we still recognize.
The ember glows, unwavering,
With each moment, nurturing.

In the depths of trust profound,
True devotion can be found.
Let the world spin and twine,
Our hearts will always align.

## Garden of Unfading Blooms

In the heart, a garden grows,
Where the gentle love still flows.
Petals soft, in colors bold,
Stories shared, forever told.

With each dawn, a new delight,
Nurtured by the morning light.
Rooted deep, we stand as one,
In this place where dreams are spun.

Upon the breeze, sweet scents arise,
Whispers hushed beneath the skies.
In this haven, time stands still,
Sowing seeds of love at will.

Though seasons change and time erodes,
Our garden still bestows its loads.
In every bloom, a memory,
A tapestry of you and me.

With every petal that we share,
We create a bond so rare.
In this garden, hand in hand,
Together, we will ever stand.

## Ties That Bind Beyond Horizon

Across the vast and endless skies,
Our spirits soar, no need for ties.
A bond that stretches far and wide,
Connected at the heart, our guide.

Through valleys low and mountains high,
In laughter's echo, we will fly.
No borders break what we hold dear,
In every moment, you are near.

With every challenge that we face,
We weave our dreams in warm embrace.
No distance can our souls unnerv,
In unity, we find our verve.

Like rivers flow, we drift as one,
Chasing rays of setting sun.
In twilight's glow, our laughter rings,
Eternal joy, this love it brings.

Though horizons may seem far away,
In every dawn, we find our way.
Boundless love, an endless tide,
In heart and spirit, we abide.

## Strength in Vulnerability

In the quiet of our fears,
We find the courage to draw near.
Soft hearts brave the stormy night,
Shining brightly, a guiding light.

With every tear that falls in grace,
We learn to hold a sacred space.
Through cracks, the brightest colors show,
Embracing all we are, we grow.

The strength we find in sharing pain,
Builds a bond that will remain.
In open arms, we softly stand,
Together facing what life planned.

A whisper brings us closer still,
In tender hearts, we find our will.
Strength in being soft and true,
In vulnerability, we renew.

In our shared journeys, we rise,
Through the heartache, beyond the skies.
Hand in hand, we pave the way,
Finding light in every day.

## A Tapestry of Trust

Threads of laughter, woven tight,
Bound in darkness, stitched in light.
Each story shared, a color blends,
In this tapestry, love transcends.

With every knot, our hearts embrace,
In every seam, there's a warm trace.
Trust is built with every thread,
A beautiful journey that lies ahead.

Through storms and calm, we intertwine,
Every moment, a sacred sign.
Fragile fibers, yet they hold,
A bond more precious than fine gold.

In gentle whispers, we confide,
With open hearts, we turn the tide.
Woven together, vibrant and bold,
A tapestry of stories told.

In trust, we find the strength to soar,
With every thread, we're bound to explore.
A fabric rich, in love we bask,
In this weave of life, we dare to ask.

## Weathered by Time

Like ancient trees that stretch and sway,
Weathered by time, they gently stay.
Roots run deep in earth's embrace,
Holding memories, a timeless space.

Seasons change, we bend and break,
But through it all, our hearts awake.
Leaves may fall, but buds will bloom,
In every challenge, we find room.

Stories told in bark and ring,
Echoes of love that time will bring.
In every scar, a chapter unfolds,
Of trials faced, and joys retold.

The passage of time, a silent guide,
In every hour, we learn to ride.
Like rivers flow in gentle sighs,
They carve the land, reflect the skies.

Weathered by time, we stand so tall,
Through ups and downs, we shall not fall.
With every sunset, a dawn will rise,
In timeless grace, we realize.

## Imprints of Togetherness

In laughter shared, our souls align,
Footprints marked in the soft pine.
Each moment captured, a gentle trace,
Imprints left in a sacred space.

Through whispered dreams, we find our way,
Together coloring the bright day.
With every heartbeat, love's embrace,
In this togetherness, we find grace.

Hand in hand, we journey forth,
Finding joy in life's true worth.
Through every challenge, we will stand,
With love, together, we are grand.

In the quiet times, we grow strong,
With melodies that feel like song.
Echoes linger in the air,
Imprints woven, everywhere.

Together we rise, together we fall,
In unity, we answer the call.
These imprints tell our story so,
In love's embrace, forever we'll glow.

## The Power of Resolve

In shadows deep, we find our light,
With steadfast hearts, we face the fight.
Though tempests roar and doubts arise,
We stand our ground, we reach the skies.

Each step we take, a choice to make,
With burning will, we will not break.
The path may twist, the journey long,
Yet in our hearts, we stay so strong.

Through trials fierce, we carve our way,
With every dawn, we greet the day.
A burning fire in every soul,
Together we rise, united, whole.

The mountains high, the valleys low,
With every challenge, we'll surely grow.
In unity, our spirits soar,
The power of resolve, forever more.

In whispers soft and courage loud,
We stand as one, we make us proud.
For in our hearts, we'll always find,
The strength to leave the past behind.

## Raindrops of Loyalty

In every storm, we find our way,
Through pouring rain, we choose to stay.
As raindrops fall, they mix and blend,
In loyalty, our hearts will mend.

With every drop, a promise made,
In sunshine bright or during shade.
We gather close, through thick and thin,
In friendship's warmth, we find our kin.

Like rivers flow, we'll never part,
Connected deep, through every heart.
In laughter shared and tears that fall,
We rise together, answering the call.

As tides may change and seasons fade,
Our bonds will last, they won't evade.
Each moment shared, a treasure true,
In raindrops of loyalty, me and you.

Through thunder's roar and lightning's flash,
In stormy skies, our spirits clash.
But hand in hand, we face the night,
With loyalty, our souls ignited.

## Diamonds of Dedication

In the depths of toil, we strive and seek,
With hearts of fire, we dare to speak.
Through sweat and tears, we carve our fate,
In dedication, we elevate.

Each challenge met, a lesson learned,
With every passion, our spirits burned.
Through darkest nights and brightest days,
We shine like diamonds in myriad ways.

Our purpose clear, our vision bright,
We chase the stars, we grasp the light.
With fervor deep, we chase our dreams,
In dedication, our spirit beams.

As time unfolds and paths align,
Together we rise, through every sign.
In every task, we'll find our place,
With diamonds of dedication, we embrace.

With steadfast hearts, we take our stand,
Through trials faced, hand in hand.
For in this journey, we dare to soar,
In dedication, we ask for more.

## Threads of Belonging

In woven tales, our stories bind,
With threads of love, we seek and find.
In every heart, a place to start,
In threads of belonging, we share our art.

Through laughter bright and sorrow's sigh,
In every moment, we reach the sky.
Connected souls in a grand design,
In threads of belonging, our lives align.

From different paths, we came together,
In every storm, in every weather.
Through trials faced, our spirits cling,
With threads of belonging, we laugh and sing.

The tapestry rich with colors true,
In every hue, I find you too.
In woven dreams, we grow and thrive,
In threads of belonging, we feel alive.

As seasons shift and years unfold,
In every heart, a story told.
Through every bond, we ever long,
With threads of belonging, we always belong.

**A Bridge of Endless Love**

Across the river, hearts unite,
A bridge of love, shining bright.
With every step, we find our way,
In each other's arms, we choose to stay.

Through storms and whispers, we will stand,
Together we dream, hand in hand.
The path is long, but we are bold,
Our story, a treasure yet untold.

In laughter and tears, we build, we grow,
Like rivers that flow, our love will show.
With grace and trust, we'll weather the tide,
In each other's hearts, forever confide.

Sunsets glow, painting the skies,
In your gaze, a world that flies.
With every dawn, our love will rise,
In endless whispers, our souls harmonize.

Together we soar, our spirits entwined,
In the dance of life, true love we find.
A bridge of endless love we share,
With every heartbeat, a sacred prayer.

## Unfading Pledges

Under the stars, our vows we speak,
In the silence, our hearts seek.
Unfading pledges, forever true,
In every moment, I cherish you.

Through shifting sands, through time's embrace,
Together we flourish, we find our place.
No mountain too high, no valley too deep,
In the promise we hold, love’s eternal leap.

Each glance a promise, each touch a seal,
In the warmth of your arms, the truth is revealed.
With whispered words, our spirits ignite,
In the shadows, you are my light.

We weather the storms, stand brave and tall,
In the tapestry of us, we weave it all.
Unfading pledges, steadfast and bold,
In the warmth of our love, a story unfolds.

Moments we treasure, memories sweet,
In this dance of love, our hearts beat.
Unfading allusions, a bond we know,
In every heartbeat, our colors glow.

## Resonance of Togetherness

In the rhythm of hearts, we find our song,
A resonance of love, where we belong.
With every beat, we dance as one,
In the glow of dawn, our journey begun.

Through whispered dreams and laughter bright,
We navigate days, embracing the light.
In the symphony of souls, we are free,
Together we rise, just you and me.

In moments shared, our spirits entwine,
With every glance, our hearts align.
The beauty in silence, the magic in words,
In the comfort of you, my heart gently stirs.

Hand in hand, we traverse the night,
In the moon's soft glow, we take flight.
Resonance of love, a sweet serenade,
In each tender moment, our fears will fade.

With laughter, we echo through every space,
In the warmth of your smile, I find grace.
Together forever, side by side,
In the journey of love, we take pride.

## The Bond Beyond Measure

In your eyes, the universe lies,
A bond beyond measure, where love never dies.
Each heartbeat a promise, glowing so bright,
In your arms, I find my light.

Time may pass, but we remain,
Through joy and sorrow, through pleasure and pain.
With you, I've found my truest friend,
In the tapestry of life, love has no end.

We navigate paths, both near and far,
In every journey, you are my star.
With every whisper, our promises we share,
In the bond beyond measure, we deeply care.

Through trials and triumphs, we will stand,
In the heart's quiet, we both understand.
With hands intertwined, we face each day,
In the bond beyond measure, come what may.

In laughter and tears, in moments of grace,
Together we thrive, in love's embrace.
In every heartbeat, our spirits soar,
The bond beyond measure, forever more.

## Vows Woven in Time

In whispers soft, our promises bind,
A tapestry rich, where hearts unwind.
Through seasons swift, our love will grow,
In every thread, the truth will flow.

With morning light, we'll chase the dawn,
As shadows fade, we carry on.
Each moment shared, a stitch so fine,
Together, we weave, our lives entwined.

The years may pass, but we'll remain,
Two souls as one, in joy and pain.
With gentle hands, we craft our fate,
Each vow a star, our love innate.

Through storms that rage, we'll find our way,
In every trial, we choose to stay.
In silence deep, our hearts will speak,
A bond so strong, no love's too weak.

So take my hand, through space and time,
In every heartbeat, your soul is mine.
With every promise, let us renew,
In this grand weave, I am with you.

## Anchored Souls

In stormy seas, our hearts stand strong,
Two anchored souls, where we belong.
With steady grace, we brave the tide,
In unity, there's naught to hide.

Through tempests fierce, we find our light,
In darkest moments, we hold tight.
With every wave, our roots go deep,
In whispered dreams, our faith we keep.

Upon this journey, side by side,
Our love, a compass, a constant guide.
With every trial, our spirits soar,
Through endless tides, we long for more.

In tranquil waters, we find our peace,
Where every heartbeat brings release.
With hearts as one, we chart our course,
In every laugh, in every source.

As seasons change, our sails remain,
The wind may shift, but love's the same.
In this vast ocean, we've cast our role,
Together forever, two anchored souls.

## Embracing Forever

In twilight's glow, our shadows blend,
A dance of time, where beginnings mend.
With open hearts, we come alive,
In every breath, our dreams will thrive.

Through whispered nights, our spirits embrace,
In every glance, a sacred space.
With gentle words, the stars align,
In love's warm cradle, our souls entwine.

In morning's light, we rise anew,
With each sunrise, my heart finds you.
Through endless days, our laughter sings,
In every moment, true love brings.

With hopeful dreams, we sail the skies,
In every kiss, eternity lies.
Through life's embrace, we'll journey on,
In every heartbeat, the past is gone.

So take my hand, let time unfold,
In love's embrace, we'll never grow old.
With every promise, forever near,
In this warm glow, I hold you dear.

## Threads of Loyalty

In every glance, a promise shared,
With threads of loyalty, we're ensnared.
Through trials faced, our bond won't fray,
In love's embrace, we find our way.

With every trial, we stand so tall,
In muted whispers, our fears will fall.
Through darkest nights, we hold the flame,
In faithful hearts, we'll stake our claim.

With gentle hands, we weave our fate,
Through winding paths, we celebrate.
In laughter bright, our spirits soar,
In threads of loyalty, we ask for more.

Through every storm, we dance as one,
In sunlight's glow, our hearts have spun.
With each sweet stitch, our memories grow,
In woven dreams, our love will flow.

So here we stand, through thick and thin,
In threads of loyalty, we shall begin.
With every heartbeat, a vow so grand,
In this rich tapestry, hand in hand.

## Love’s Sacred Oath

In whispered night, we pledge our hearts,
A bond unbroken, never departs.
With every breath, our spirits blend,
A sacred oath, love knows no end.

Together we stand, in shadows and light,
Facing the storms, holding on tight.
Through laughter and tears, we share our days,
In each other's eyes, forever stays.

With gentle hands, we carve our way,
In a world that spins, come what may.
Our souls entwined, like vines that grow,
In love’s embrace, we’ll always glow.

As seasons change, and time moves on,
In every sunset, our love’s reborn.
Through trials faced, and dreams we share,
A sacred bond beyond compare.

So here we stand, in truth and grace,
With love’s sweet oath in this sacred space.
Two hearts entwined, forever free,
In endless love, just you and me.

## Harmonies of Unity

In melodies soft, we find our way,
A symphony of hearts, come what may.
Together we dance, to the music divine,
In harmonies sweet, our souls align.

Through every note, our spirits soar,
United in love, we seek for more.
In laughter and joy, we share our song,
A chorus of unity, where we belong.

With every heartbeat, the rhythm flows,
In a world of chaos, together we pose.
In quiet moments, our silence sings,
A tapestry woven with invisible strings.

As seasons change, our song remains,
In every struggle, love sustains.
Through trials faced, we rise above,
In the harmonies crafted from endless love.

Together we write this melody grand,
With notes of hope, hand in hand.
In unity found, we sing our truth,
In life's grand orchestra, our blossomed youth.

## Pillars of Endurance

In strength we stand, like ancient stone,
Pillars of love, never alone.
Through storms that rage, and winds that blow,
In unity forged, together we grow.

With every challenge, we rise anew,
Bound by the love that sees us through.
In moments of doubt, we gather might,
With hearts as one, we face the night.

As time etches lines upon our face,
In each scar, a testament of grace.
Through trials we've faced, our spirits strong,
In pillars of trust, we both belong.

With courage bold, we walk this line,
In every heartbeat, your hand in mine.
Through valleys deep, we dare to tread,
In the light of hope, our fears are shed.

So here we stand, side by side,
In love's embrace, with nothing to hide.
Pillars of endurance, forever we'll be,
In this journey of life, just you and me.

## Echoes of Vows

In sacred whispers, our vows take flight,
Echoes of promises, shining bright.
With every heartbeat, we pledge our fate,
In love's own story, it's never too late.

Through each dawn's light, our vows renew,
In every laughter, every tear too.
With hands held tight, we face the unknown,
In echoes of love, our seeds are sown.

As moments pass, we gather the years,
In echoes of joy, and even our fears.
For in every step, our spirits dance,
In love's sweet song, we take our chance.

As twilight falls, our hearts are one,
In whispers of love, when day is done.
Echoes of vows, through time they flow,
In the heart's deep chambers, our love will grow.

So let us cherish, this bond we hold,
In echoes of warmth, more precious than gold.
Together we journey, hand in hand,
In the echoes of vows, forever we stand.

## Hands Held Through Time

In the quiet of night, we stand still,
Holding dreams that our hearts fulfill.
With each whispered wish, we intertwine,
A bond as strong as the endless vine.

Through laughter and tears, we've grown wise,
In the dance of life, under vast skies.
Through trials faced and joys we find,
Our hands remain held, forever aligned.

In moments shared, both bright and dim,
We soar to heights, our love the hymn.
Time flows gently, as rivers bend,
Together we journey, no start or end.

As seasons change and years unfold,
Our tale is written, in skies of gold.
In the garden of life, we plant each seed,
Hands held through time, our hearts take the lead.

## Melodies of Deep Affection

Soft notes linger in the evening air,
Dancing melodies, a love we share.
Each chord a whisper, sweet and clear,
In this song of hearts, I hold you near.

Through symphonies bright and soft refrains,
Our spirits entwined, like gentle rains.
With every heartbeat, a rhythm divine,
Together we sway, your hand in mine.

The world fades away as we sing on,
In this serenade, we feel so strong.
Our laughter echoes, a radiant sound,
In the music of love, we are unbound.

Under the stars, our chorus takes flight,
Melodies woven in the soft moonlight.
With each note played, our stories align,
In this orchestra of love, you are mine.

## Stones Carved by Loyalty

In the mountains high, our promise stands,
Like stones carved deep by gentle hands.
Time and weather shape every line,
A testament fierce, our hearts align.

Through storms we weathered, side by side,
In loyalty's grip, we take great pride.
Each challenge faced, we've stood as one,
Chiseled in faith, our love has begun.

In whispers of wind, our story is told,
Of a bond unyielding, steadfast and bold.
As ages pass, we will not sway,
Like stones intertwined, forever we stay.

Roots in the earth, we grow ever strong,
In the fabric of time, we each belong.
Through valleys low, and peaks that gleam,
Our loyalty flows, a shared dream.

## The Journey We Share

With each step taken, side by side,
Through winding paths, we feel the glide.
In moments fleeting, and dreams anew,
Together we wander, just me and you.

Over mountains high and rivers wide,
In this journey of life, we take great pride.
Hand in hand, we chart our course,
With love as our guide, a powerful force.

Through valleys of doubt, and skies of blue,
In every heartbeat, I find you true.
As time unwinds, our spirits soar,
Each footstep echoes, forevermore.

With laughter as our map, and love our light,
We travel together, from day into night.
In the tapestry of moments we weave,
The journey we share, our hearts believe.

## Stars Aligned in Trust

In the night sky, dreams collide,
Constellations draw us near.
Each twinkle a promise, a guide,
In the silence, we conquer fear.

Hand in hand, we chase the light,
Our hopes reflected in the stars.
Together, we embrace the night,
Boundless love heals all our scars.

Through dark paths, we tread with grace,
Time will test our steadfast bond.
But trust will always find its place,
In every shadow, we're beyond.

The universe sings our tune,
A symphony of faith and dreams.
Beneath this vast, eternal moon,
Our souls entwined, love redeems.

Stars aligned, fate weaves its thread,
In the fabric of our trust.
In every heartbeat, words unsaid,
In this love, we find we must.

## Emblems of Enduring Love

Through seasons change, our story grows,
In whispers sweet, our hearts take flight.
Enduring love, like river flows,
A timeless dance, both bold and bright.

Upon the canvas, memories paint,
Each stroke a testament of claim.
In tender moments, no room for faint,
Emblems of love, we carve our name.

With every dawn, a chance reborn,
In laughter shared, in tears we mend.
Together weather, fight the storm,
In every challenge, we won't bend.

Our hands entwined, in silent prayer,
Vows spoken softly, hearts laid bare.
In every heartbeat, I am there,
Enduring love, a treasure rare.

From dusk till dawn, through thick and thin,
With each embrace, our bond will bloom.
In love's sweet dance, we find the win,
Two souls as one, dispelling gloom.

## Whispers in the Fog

Beneath the veil of morning mist,
Soft murmurs guide our way ahead.
In secret glades, where shadows twist,
Whispers linger, words unsaid.

With every step, our spirits soar,
Through tangled trees, we find our ground.
In love's embrace, we seek for more,
In the silence, hope resounds.

The fog may hide what lies in view,
Yet in the soft glow, hearts unite.
Together, we chase the dew,
As dawn unveils the path of light.

In laughter shared beneath the haze,
We find the strength to walk this road.
Through whispered songs that gently blaze,
Our trust in love becomes our code.

So hand in hand, we brave the chill,
With every shadow, light will break.
In whispers soft, our dreams fulfill,
Together, we awake, we wake.

## A Pathway Paved in Trust

In the journey, steps align,
Each moment shared, a treasure found.
Through winding paths, your hand in mine,
We walk together, love profound.

With every turn, our hearts will guide,
In starry nights and sun-drenched days.
Through storms and trials, side by side,
A pathway paved, love never sways.

With open hearts, we face the road,
The weight of worries washed away.
In trust, our souls share every load,
In gentle whispers, fears decay.

Each mile we tread, a story spun,
In laughter, tears, we dream anew.
In every challenge, we become one,
A bond unbreakable, fierce and true.

So here's to journeys yet to start,
With faith as our steadfast steer.
In every beat, you fill my heart,
With you, my love, there’s nothing to fear.

## Hearts in Concert

Two souls entwined, a melody shared,
In the rhythm of time, emotions bared.
Through whispers soft, love's notes arise,
A symphony dances beneath the skies.

Fingers touch, a gentle embrace,
Moments where stillness finds its place.
Together we soar, our spirits aligned,
In this concert of hearts, true joy we find.

Each heartbeat echoes, a song of its own,
In harmony's grip, we've never felt lone.
With laughter as chords and dreams intertwined,
In this grand orchestration, our souls combined.

Facing the storms, we will not part,
In every dark note, you're the light in my heart.
Through crescendo and pause, our love is defined,
Together, forever, our fates intertwined.

As the curtain falls on this beautiful scene,
With love as our guide, we have forever gleaned.
With every encore, anew we will start,
For our lives are a concert, united in heart.

## Flame of Resolute Affection

In the still of night, a spark ignites,
A flame of love that fiercely bites.
Through winds that howl and shadows that sway,
Together we stand, come what may.

With every glance, the fire grows bright,
In soft whispered words, we find our light.
Through seasons that change and skies that weep,
Our love's a promise, forever to keep.

With each trial met, the blaze won't die,
In the depths of our hearts, we dare to fly.
Even through storms that test our way,
Our resolute passion will always stay.

A dance of embers, warmth in the night,
In the embrace of each other, we find our might.
With faith as our shield and dreams in our sight,
We're bound by this flame, a beautiful rite.

As time drifts on, the hearth remains,
In the glow of affection, love never wanes.
With a flicker of hope and a heart that believes,
Our flame of affection, forever achieves.

## The Art of Lasting Promises

In quiet moments, promises bloom,
Like fragile petals, dispelling the gloom.
Binding our fates with every vow,
In the art of love, we expertly bow.

Through valleys low and mountains high,
We stand together, never shy.
Every word spoken, each heartfelt pledge,
A canvas of trust, we carefully hedge.

With colors of joy and strokes of pain,
We paint our future, sunshine and rain.
In the gallery of hearts, our memories live,
The art of promises, forever we give.

As seasons dance, and years swiftly wane,
Our promises flourish, like flowers in rain.
Each moment cherished, each dream we chase,
In the tapestry woven, love finds its place.

So let us honor this oath we've made,
In every heartbeat, our love won't fade.
With a brush of affection, our lives intertwine,
In the art of lasting promises, forever we shine.

## Shadows of Faithfulness

In the twilight's hush, shadows align,
Echoes of promises, tender and fine.
With the moon as witness and stars our guide,
In faithfulness, we find where we abide.

Through trails unknown and paths untried,
In every shadow, love will bide.
In the quiet echoes of whispers sweet,
We gather strength, and our hearts repeat.

With hands held tightly, we forge the night,
In shadows of warmth, we find our light.
Through silence shared and laughter bright,
Faithfulness whispers, always in sight.

In storms that rage, our bond will persist,
Through shadows we wander, love will assist.
Each step a testament, every sigh pure,
In this sacred dance, our hearts endure.

As dawn breaks gently, with hope anew,
In shadows of faith, our love rings true.
With every promise, a light we embrace,
In shadows forever, together we grace.

## In the Embrace of Promises

In the quiet whispers of the night,
A vow was sealed, a soft delight.
Underneath the starry sky,
Hearts entwined, we dared to fly.

With every heartbeat, secrets shared,
Bound by dreams, and souls laid bare.
In the light of dawn, we rise anew,
Promises made, and love so true.

Storms may come, but here we stand,
With open hearts and steadfast hands.
Through trials, we will find our way,
In the embrace of love's warm sway.

Each moment cherished, every glance,
A dance of fate, a sweet romance.
In the garden where hope blooms bright,
We nurture dreams in morning light.

May shadows fall, but never break,
Our bond of trust, for love's own sake.
Hand in hand, through thick and thin,
In the embrace, our hearts shall win.

## Love’s Unyielding Anchor

Amidst the waves, my heart set sail,
In love's embrace, I shall not fail.
Through tempests fierce and skies of gray,
Your heart's my anchor, come what may.

In silent moments, our spirits meld,
A fortress strong, where fears are quelled.
With whispered dreams and bold intent,
Together, we are heaven-sent.

With every tide, my trust will grow,
As side by side, we ebb and flow.
For in your eyes, I find my way,
Love’s lighthouse shines both night and day.

Through storms that rage and skies that clear,
Your steady heartbeat draws me near.
No doubt can sway what we have found,
In love’s embrace, we are safe and sound.

So let the world around us quake,
In love’s warm glow, we shall not break.
For like a ship that knows the shore,
Love’s unyielding anchor, forever more.

## Chains of Affection

In the warmth of sunlit days,
Love's gentle touch sets hearts ablaze.
Each link we forge, steady and strong,
Chains of affection where we belong.

Through laughter shared and tears we shed,
On this journey, there's love to spread.
Every moment, a treasure rare,
In the chains of affection, love is fair.

With every spark, our spirits dance,
In the rhythm of this sweet romance.
Bound together by hopes and dreams,
Love's radiant light forever gleams.

In the shadows, we find our way,
Through the night and into the day.
Each challenge met, we rise above,
Strong and united, forged in love.

So here we stand, no end in sight,
In the hardest battles, we will fight.
For in these chains, our hearts entwine,
In the bonds of affection, forever shine.

## Glimmers of Fidelity

In the twilight, soft and sweet,
Our love's a glow, a rhythmic beat.
Each glance we share ignites the skies,
Glimmers of fidelity in our eyes.

With tender words, we cross the miles,
In every hug, a thousand smiles.
Through every trial, we stand as one,
Two hearts united, never undone.

In gentle whispers, promises bloom,
A sacred bond that’s free from gloom.
With trust as our guiding star,
Glimmers of fidelity, near and far.

Through seasons changing, we will stay,
In each other's arms, come what may.
Our souls are linked, a timeless flame,
In love's embrace, we shall not wane.

So as the years begin to fade,
Through life's vast seas, our course is laid.
Together we’ll sail, strong and free,
In glimmers of fidelity, you and me.

## Promises Wrapped in Silence

In whispers soft, we make our vows,
A secret bond the heart endows.
Through muted words, our souls entwine,
In silence sweet, our love does shine.

With every sigh, a promise sworn,
In the quiet dusk, our dreams are born.
Each glance a pledge, each touch a seal,
In this stillness, our truths reveal.

The world may fade, but here we stand,
In silent grace, we hold each hand.
Though storms may come, we'll find our way,
In the hush, our hearts will stay.

We weave our hopes like threads of gold,
In silent tales, our love unfolds.
No need for words to paint the scene,
In silence, love is felt and seen.

Thus, in this quiet, we remain,
Wrapped in promises, free of pain.
In every pause, our hearts align,
In whispered dreams, our love divine.

## Vows Under Starry Skies

Beneath the stars, our hearts collide,
In the night's embrace, we bide.
With every twinkle, a promise glows,
In the vastness, our love grows.

We speak in glimpses, in silent trusts,
On this night, our hearts combust.
Each constellation, a vow so bright,
In the cosmic dance, we take flight.

The moon bears witness to our plight,
In shadows cast, we find our light.
With hands entwined, we dream anew,
In the starlit skies, our love rings true.

Around us swirls the night's embrace,
In this vast cosmos, we find our place.
No need for words to share our fates,
In the universe, our love creates.

As dawn approaches, we hold on tight,
To this night's whispers, pure and right.
With hearts aglow, we face the day,
In night's soft light, we'll find our way.

## Oath of the Unwavering

With steadfast hearts, we take our stand,
In storms and calm, we'll never disband.
With every vow, our spirits soar,
In unity, we'll rise and explore.

Through trials faced and shadows cast,
Our love endures, an anchor vast.
In every challenge, we find our fire,
With courage deep, we'll climb higher.

A beacon bright in darkest night,
Together we blaze with purest light.
Each oath we share, a bond profound,
In loyalty's heart, our dreams are found.

With unwavering faith, we press ahead,
On this path, our souls are fed.
Through every trial, our hearts entwine,
In strength anew, our love will shine.

In every leap and every fall,
Together we rise, we stand tall.
With love so true, we navigate,
In faith we flourish, we celebrate.

## Bonds Woven in Time

In threads of gold, our story's spun,
With every moment, two become one.
Through seasons change, our roots run deep,
In laughter shared, our memories keep.

Each year that passes, new tales are told,
In the fabric of life, our hearts hold.
With every stitch, we craft our fate,
In love's embrace, we celebrate.

Through tides of time, we ebb and flow,
In the canvas we paint, our love will grow.
With every dawn, a fresh design,
In the loom of life, our hearts align.

The threads may fray, the colors fade,
Yet in this tapestry, love won't jade.
With every heartbeat, together we strive,
In this woven bond, we thrive.

So let the years unfurl like a scroll,
In the dance of time, we play our role.
With hands held tight, we weave our rhyme,
In every heartbeat, bonds woven in time.

## In the Light of Devotion

In shadows deep, a heart stands tall,
With every whisper, love's sweet call.
Through trials faced, we stand as one,
In the light of devotion, our journey's begun.

Hands clasped tight, we face the night,
Guided by stars, our dreams take flight.
In moments of doubt, we find our way,
For love's gentle beacon will never sway.

With patience fierce, we hold the flame,
In every heartbeat, we call your name.
Through storms we weather, together we shine,
In the light of devotion, your heart is mine.

With quiet vows, we choose to rise,
Building a world where truth defies.
In every glance, a promise bestowed,
In the light of devotion, our love will explode.

Radiant wishes, dreams unfurled,
Two souls intertwine in this vast world.
In the glow of our hope, we find our strength,
In the light of devotion, we go the length.

## Wings of Unwavering Trust

In the quiet dawn, we take to flight,
With wings of trust, hearts shining bright.
Through valleys low and mountains high,
Together we soar, just you and I.

With every challenge, we learn to bend,
In the winds of fate, we find a friend.
Guided by faith, through storms we sail,
Wings of unwavering trust will never fail.

Though shadows may cast, and doubts may creep,
In the embrace of love, our dreams we keep.
On this journey's edge, we write our song,
With wings of unwavering trust, we are strong.

Each moment shared, a treasure rare,
In the heart's quiet, we find our care.
To believe in each other, come what may,
Wings of unwavering trust light our way.

In the tapestry of life, a bond so true,
With open hearts, we'll break through.
In every step, in every gust,
We rise together on wings of trust.

## Knots Tied in Love

In a world of chaos, we find our peace,
Knots tied in love, our hearts release.
With tender ties, we weave our fate,
In every embrace, we celebrate.

Through seasons that change, we hold on tight,
In laughter and tears, we find our light.
With every promise, our spirits align,
Knots tied in love, beautifully entwined.

In whispers shared, our secrets bloom,
Within these ties, we find our room.
Through trials faced, we are made strong,
Knots tied in love will carry us long.

With gentle strength and fearless will,
We conquer doubts, our hearts to fill.
As life unfolds, in every heartbeat,
Knots tied in love, our journey complete.

So here's to the ties that never fray,
In the warmth of love, we find our way.
With each knot tightened, our roots run deep,
In knots tied in love, our souls will leap.

## A Symphony of Connection

In the stillness, a melody flows,
A symphony of hearts, as love bestows.
With every note, a story unfolds,
In a harmony rich, our truth retold.

Through laughter bright and sorrows shared,
In moments cherished, our souls are bared.
With every chord, we dance as one,
A symphony of connection, forever begun.

In the echoes of time, our spirits rise,
In the beauty of this, we recognize.
With every beat, our love takes flight,
A symphony of connection, shining bright.

As seasons change, we find our tune,
In the moon's soft glow and the sun's warm noon.
With hands held tight, we change the game,
A symphony of connection, never the same.

So let us play, with hearts open wide,
In this grand composition, side by side.
For in every silence, and every sound,
A symphony of connection, forever profound.

## In the Silence of Promises

In the hush where whispers dwell,
A vow is bound, no need to tell.
Hearts entwined, where shadows play,
In silence, love finds its way.

Promises made, unspoken trust,
Like morning dew, in love we must.
In the stillness, eyes align,
Through quiet breaths, our souls combine.

Seasons change, but we remain,
In the moments, joy and pain.
Each heartbeat echoes what we feel,
In silence, a bond so real.

Fleeting words, yet strong and clear,
In the silence, you are near.
Promises whispered, never lost,
In love's embrace, we pay the cost.

In the echoes of the night,
A lasting pledge, softly bright.
Together we weave, thread so fine,
In the silence, your hand in mine.

## A Chorus of Belief

In the dawn, where dreams take flight,
Voices rise, a shared delight.
With every note, a story spun,
Together strong, we are as one.

Harmony in every heart,
In this symphony, we play our part.
The world may dim, the storms may sway,
But our belief will light the way.

Through trials faced and laughter shared,
In every chord, we've always cared.
A chorus built on trust and grace,
In unity, we find our place.

When hope feels lost, and shadows creep,
Our melody shall rise, not sleep.
With every note, we claim our chance,
In this chorus, we shall dance.

Together as the seasons change,
In every sound, we rearrange.
This harmony, forever true,
In belief, I stand with you.

## Foundations of Togetherness

With roots entwined in fertile ground,
We build our dreams where love is found.
Each brick a memory, a shared embrace,
In the foundation, a sacred space.

Through laughter shared and trials faced,
We carve our mark, no time is wasted.
With every challenge, stronger we grow,
In togetherness, our joys overflow.

Hands joined tight in every storm,
In the warmth of each other, we stay warm.
The path ahead may twist and bend,
But side by side, we will defend.

A tapestry stitched with care and love,
Nurtured beneath the stars above.
Our dreams take flight, like birds in the sky,
In foundations strong, we learn to fly.

Every moment, a step we take,
A journey forged in love's great wake.
Together we'll venture, forever bold,
In the warmth of togetherness, we find gold.

## The Language of Commitment

In words unspoken, we define,
A promise held, forever thine.
Through gestures small, our hearts align,
In commitment, our lives entwine.

Every glance, a silent vow,
In our togetherness, we take a bow.
With every choice, we write our tale,
In commitment's strength, we shall prevail.

Not just in words but in our deeds,
A garden grows from faithful seeds.
Through trials faced, we stand as one,
In the warmth of love, we've just begun.

Each day a chance to share and grow,
In the language of commitment, we show.
With hearts wide open, we bravely tread,
In love's embrace, no words unsaid.

Together we craft this life so sweet,
In every step, our hearts repeat.
The language spoken, soft yet grand,
In commitment's dance, forever we stand.

## A Canvas of Forever

In twilight hues the colors blend,
Whispers of dreams that softly send,
Brushstrokes of time on a silent stage,
Creating a tale that cannot age.

Stars paint the night with shimmering light,
Each tiny spark, a wish taking flight,
A masterpiece spanning the endless skies,
A canvas of time where love never dies.

In every shadow, a story unfolds,
In every moment, a memory holds,
Time weaves its fabric, a tapestry bright,
A canvas of forever, bathed in soft light.

Through storms and through calm, we find our way,
With strokes of our hearts, we'll ever stay,
Each hue that we mix, each shade that we share,
Brings forth a love that's eternally rare.

So take my hand and paint your dreams,
In this world of ours, where nothing redeems,
Together we'll craft the infinite scene,
On a canvas of forever, where love reigns supreme.

## The Sound of Your Name

Whispers in the breeze call out to me,
Softly they sing, like waves of the sea,
In every echo, your voice rings clear,
The sound of your name, a melody dear.

Through bustling streets and quiet nights,
Your name dances softly, igniting delights,
It lingers like perfume in the air,
A symphony played with utmost care.

In laughter shared, it calls me near,
In shadows cast, it's always here,
A rhythm that flows with each heartbeat's claim,
Forever and always, the sound of your name.

In moments of silence, it softly lingers,
Like the touch of poetry dancing on fingers,
A light in the dark, a spark in the flame,
My heart rejoices at the sound of your name.

So let me whisper it under the skies,
A song of devotion that never denies,
Each syllable precious, no one could tame,
For life is a song, and you are the frame.

## Unbroken Reflections

In the mirror's gaze, we find our truth,
Fragments of time embody our youth,
Each wrinkle a story, each scar a song,
Unbroken reflections where we belong.

In still waters deep, secrets reveal,
The heart's gentle whispers, a tender appeal,
In shadows and light, we dance with fate,
Unbroken reflections, love resonates.

Time may wear down the mask that we wear,
But within lies a beauty so rare,
With every glance, a moment replays,
Unbroken reflections in time's soft gaze.

Through trials and triumphs, hand in hand,
We forge our path, we make our stand,
A tapestry woven with hopes and dreams,
In unbroken reflections, love always gleams.

So let us embrace each fragment we find,
In the dance of our lives, our hearts intertwined,
For in every echo, our souls will relay,
Unbroken reflections that never decay.

## Roots of Eternal Love

Deep in the earth, where the wildflowers grow,
Lie roots intertwined, a secret we sow,
Through storms that may come, we hold our ground,
Roots of eternal love, forever bound.

Each season that passes, a test of our might,
Yet together we flourish, reaching new height,
In shadows of doubt, our bond shines bright,
Like stars in the velvet, a guiding light.

With every heartbeat, our spirits entwined,
In fields where we laughed, our past is defined,
Winds whisper our tale, like a love song sung,
Roots of eternal love, forever young.

Through trials that challenge and dreams that arise,
We'll conquer the mountains, we'll touch the skies,
In the garden of life, where we've lovingly trod,
Roots of eternal love, nurtured by God.

So let the world wander, let the seasons change,
Our love is the anchor, it will not estrange,
In the heart of the earth, our bond holds tight,
Roots of eternal love, an everlasting light.

## Shadows Cast by Steadfast Souls

In twilight's glow, we stand so near,
With whispers soft, we shed our fear.
Beneath the stars, our dreams take flight,
Two steady hearts, embraced by night.

In every shadow, love resides,
Through silent storms, our truth abides.
The paths we tread, though dark and wide,
Together still, we will not hide.

Our voices blend, a sacred song,
In harmony, where we belong.
With steadfast souls, we face the dawn,
Through every dusk, our bond goes on.

In shadows cast, the light may fade,
But in our hearts, the fire's made.
We journey forth, hand in hand tight,
In life's deep realms, still, we ignite.

From dusk to dawn, in joy and strife,
We write our story, weave through life.
With every breath, our pact is sealed,
In the shadows, our truth revealed.

## The Language of Untold Promises

In silence, words remain unspoken,
A tender bond that won’t be broken.
With every glance, a tale unfolds,
Of love that shines, of hearts so bold.

The threads we weave, though soft, entwine,
A rhythm found, a dance divine.
In secret sighs, our dreams conspire,
A language born from pure desire.

In shadows deep, our voices rise,
With whispered hopes, beneath the skies.
Each promise forged in quiet light,
Illuminates our path so bright.

Through stormy seas and calm afloat,
We sail on trust, our hearts promote.
Each untold promise, a gentle gift,
To hold, to cherish, and to lift.

In every heartbeat, echoes thrice,
The language of our sacrifice.
Together strong, we chase the dawn,
In every word, our love goes on.

## Ink of the Everlasting

With quill in hand, my heart I share,
On pages blank, your love laid bare.
Each stroke of ink, a tale engraved,
Of moments blessed, and hearts that braved.

The stories penned will never fade,
In timeless bonds, our love portrayed.
In every line, a memory spins,
The ink, it flows where true love begins.

With every verse, the world unfolds,
In whispered dreams, our truth behold.
A canvas bright, where souls align,
With ink of love, forever shines.

From dusk till dawn, the pages turn,
Through trials faced, it's you I yearn.
In written words, our hearts conjoin,
In ink of lasting, we find our joy.

Together penned, through time and space,
In every word, your soft embrace.
The story blooms, forever bold,
In ink of the everlasting told.

## Footprints on Shared Paths

Upon this road, our footprints blend,
With every step, the hearts ascend.
In laughter shared, we find our way,
Together woven, come what may.

The trails we walk, with joy we trace,
In every turn, we find our place.
Each mark we leave, a memory dear,
The whispers of love, forever near.

Through winding paths, our spirits soar,
In every heartbeat, we crave more.
With eyes alight, we chase the sun,
In shared delight, we are as one.

From mountain high to valley low,
In every season, our love will grow.
With open hearts, we greet the dawn,
In every step, our bond lives on.

Together strong, we've faced the fight,
In twilight’s glow, our souls ignite.
Embracing life, our destinies,
Footprints on paths, carried by breeze.

## Anchored in Your Embrace

In quiet nights, your warmth is near,
A shelter found, dispelling fear.
With whispered dreams that gently sway,
Your love's a light that guides my way.

Through stormy seas, we stand as one,
Together facing life’s great run.
A bond so strong, it won’t let go,
In every heart, your kindness grows.

The tides may change, but we remain,
A love that breaks the strongest chain.
With every heartbeat, I can see,
Your spirit dances, wild and free.

Hand in hand, we'll face the night,
With stars above, a perfect sight.
Your gentle touch, a sweet embrace,
In every moment, I find grace.

In laughter shared and tears we cry,
A promise whispered, never die.
In anchored hearts, we find our place,
Forever held in love’s warm space.

## A Dance of Unseen Threads

In shadowed corners, whispers blend,
A dance begins that knows no end.
With every glance, a tie so real,
Unseen threads of love we feel.

Through ages past, we've intertwined,
In every heart, our souls aligned.
A tapestry of dreams we weave,
With every sigh, we dare believe.

The music swells, the lights grow dim,
In perfect chore, we rise and swim.
A gentle tug, a soft embrace,
Together lost in time and space.

With every step, we paint the sky,
A journey bold, you and I.
In laughter's grace, in sorrows shared,
Each unseen thread is truly bared.

A dance that spirals ever on,
In silent words, we find our song.
A heartbeat close, a rhythm true,
In timeless steps, I dance with you.

## Waters of Faithful Trust

In cool embrace of waters deep,
Where dreams may swim and secrets keep.
Each ripple tells a tale of old,
In faithful trust, our hands we hold.

A quiet stream that flows so clear,
A reservoir of hope held dear.
With every wave, we rise and fall,
Together, strong, we heed the call.

In every splash, a joyful sound,
A bond so pure, forever bound.
With hearts afloat, we drift as one,
In life’s embrace, the journey’s fun.

From silver lakes to oceans wide,
In waters deep, we'll ever glide.
A faithful trust, a silent vow,
In tranquil depths, we’re anchored now.

Through patient tides that shift and flow,
In every challenge, we will grow.
In waters warm, we find our way,
Forever loved, come what may.

## Eternal Echoes of Affection

In twilight’s glow, whispers remain,
Through each heartbeat, love's gentle strain.
The echoes dance in time’s soft light,
In every shadow, love ignites.

With every sigh, my heart takes flight,
In melodies of the softest night.
A symphony of dreams we share,
In endless realms, we breathe the air.

Through mountains high and valleys low,
An endless rhythm, we both know.
With every glance, a silent song,
In echoes true, we both belong.

The stars above, they watch and gleam,
In cosmic threads, we weave the dream.
With every year, our stories blend,
Eternal echoes that won’t end.

In every beat, in every breath,
A testament that conquers death.
In love’s embrace, we find our truth,
An infinite dance of timeless youth.

## The Lantern of Faithful Hearts

In twilight's glow, we hold the light,
A flame that flickers, ever bright.
Through stormy nights and endless skies,
We guide each other, never shy.

With every step, we find our way,
In faith's embrace, we choose to stay.
Together strong, we'll face the dark,
Our hearts united, be the spark.

Each challenge met, each tear we share,
A bond unbroken, pure and rare.
In laughter's ring, in sorrow's song,
The lantern shines, where we belong.

So let us walk, this path we pave,
With hearts ablaze, let love be brave.
For in this dance, we find our peace,
A faithful light that will not cease.

Embracing faith, through thick and thin,
The journey starts where love begins.
Our lanterns glow, forever bright,
In faithful hearts, we find our light.

## Songbirds of Unyielding Devotion

In morning's song, we wake anew,
Our voices blend, a vibrant hue.
With every note, our hearts take flight,
A melody that feels so right.

Through whispered winds, our spirits soar,
In harmony, we seek for more.
With treble high and bass so deep,
Together in this promise keep.

With wings of hope, we'll face the storm,
A symphony that keeps us warm.
Each phrase we sing, a treasure true,
In every chord, our love shines through.

When shadows fall, we'll not despair,
For in our hearts, we always care.
Our songbirds' call, a beacon bright,
In unyielding love, we find our light.

So let us sing, and let it be,
A testament of you and me.
In every note, forever strive,
Songbirds of love, we feel alive.

## The Canvas of Cherished Days

With every brush, we paint our past,
In colors bright, our memories cast.
Each stroke a moment, etched in time,
A vivid tale, a silent rhyme.

The laughter echoes, shadows play,
In every hue, a cherished day.
With golden sunsets, skies of blue,
We weave a fabric, strong and true.

Through seasons' change, we find our grace,
In every line, a warm embrace.
The canvas holds our hopes and dreams,
A masterpiece, or so it seems.

Through trials faced, our colors blend,
In every heart, a loyal friend.
So let us paint with love's own light,
Creating beauty, day and night.

Together here, let's add our shade,
Each memory made, will never fade.
On this canvas, where we belong,
Our cherished days, forever strong.

## Serene Strength of Togetherness

In quiet moments, hand in hand,
We find the strength to take a stand.
With gentle hearts and minds aligned,
A bond unbroken, deeply intertwined.

Through life's great waves, we navigate,
In trust's embrace, we celebrate.
With every challenge, we will rise,
Together strong, we touch the skies.

In laughter's warmth and sorrow's shade,
We've built a world that will not fade.
With every step, we face the fray,
In unity, we'll find the way.

With steady hearts, we share the load,
In every moment, love bestowed.
Together here, we learn and grow,
In serene strength, our spirits glow.

So let us walk, this path as one,
In every dusk, we'll meet the sun.
For in togetherness, we thrive,
A journey rich, we come alive.

Printed in the USA
CPSIA information can be obtained
at www.ICGtesting.com
LVHW021922021024
792764LV00012B/158

9 789916 893203